TRAVELER'S GUIDE TO WISCONSIN'S LAKE SUPERIOR SHORE

I0151093

COVERING THE TOWNS OF ASHLAND, WASHBURN, BAYFIELD, RED CLIFF, CORNUCOPIA AND THE SURROUNDING AREA

Lawrence Newman

Traveler's Guide To Wisconsin's Lake Superior Shore

Copyright © 2021 by Lawrence Newman

ISBN 978-0-9885553-5-8

Library of Congress Control Number: 2013921871

Printed in the United States of America

Seventh Edition

Publisher: Silver Millennium Publications, Inc.
          Gold Canyon, Arizona

Front cover photo: View from the 3rd tee of the Apostle Highlands Golf Course

Other books by the author

The Apostle Islands—America's Wilderness In The Water

Discovering The Apostle Islands

Sailing Adventures In The Apostle Islands

Tales Of A Nautical Novice:
Lessons I Learned Boating In The Great Lakes

1000 Outstanding Quotes You Should Know

Treasury of "On Target" Humorous Quotes For Public Speakers

Motivational Quotes For Coaches, Captains and Team Leaders

Self-Publishing Your Book: A Nuts and Bolts Approach

Wish I'd Said That: Quotes You Won't Forget

Dedicated to Christine,
my wife and lifelong companion,
who always supported me

TO THE READER

After writing three books on the Apostle Islands it became obvious to me that a book, aimed at visitors coming to the Lake Superior shore of Wisconsin, would also be useful.

Although visitors could make inquiries of local businesses and the local Chambers of Commerce, finding answers to many of their questions, it's possible that they might not be aware of many of the recreational opportunities and sights available in the area, or have the time to discover them.

I've been coming to this area of northern Wisconsin for over fifty years. My father was born in Ashland in 1909 and our family spent two-week vacations up here starting back in the early 1940's. I now spend much of the summer months in my home east of Ashland, which gives me the opportunity to continue to participate in many of the activities available in the area. In addition to a little fishing and boating in Chequamegon Bay I am also able to do some sailing among the islands.

In the pages that follow I have attempted to give the summer visitor to Wisconsin's northern shore a quick overview of the activities available. I've also included my recommended places to dine at or visit. There are many other fine stores and restaurants that are worth your time, but space limitations prevented me from mentioning them all. The local Chambers of Commerce will provide information on many of these businesses.

I hope you can spend the time to visit and appreciate this beautiful area of Wisconsin situated on the largest fresh water lake in the world.

L. Newman
January 14, 2021

TRAVELER'S GUIDE TO WISCONSIN'S LAKE SUPERIOR SHORE

TABLE OF CONTENTS

General Comments—A Quick Overview............ 1

From the Michigan Border to Ashland….......… 5

Ashland—Lake Superior's Hometown............. 7

From Ashland to Washburn........................... 29

Washburn—A Small Town on the Greatest Lake. 32

From Washburn to Bayfield........................... 37

Bayfield—Gateway to the Apostle Islands......... 43

Historic La Pointe on Madeline Island.............. 55

From Bayfield to Cornucopia.......................... 59

Cornucopia.. 63

From Cornucopia to the Minnesota Border........ 66

Appendix I Lake Superior Facts.................... 71

Appendix II History of the Area...................... 73

Appendix III The Kennedy Connection............. 80

Appendix IV Historic Milestones of Ashland...... 83

Sources for Additional Information:

Apostle Islands............................... 86
Area Information............................. 87
Big Top Chautauqua.......................... 88
Camping—National Lakeshore.............. 88
Campgrounds................................. 88
Cruise Boats, Water Taxis, Ferry............. 89
Fishing Charters............................... 90
Hiking... 91
Kayaks/Canoes............................... 92
Kennedy Connection.......................... 93
Lighthouses................................... 93
Museums...................................... 94
National Park Service......................... 94
Native American History...................... 95
Northern Great Lakes Visitor Center......... 95
Restaurants................................... 95
Sailboat Charters-Bareboat................... 96
Sailboat Charters-Captained.................. 96

TRAVELER'S GUIDE TO WISCONSIN'S LAKE SUPERIOR SHORE

General Comments—A Quick Overview

This book's itinerary of recommended stops along Wisconsin's northern shore follows an east to west route beginning at the Wisconsin/Michigan border and proceeding to the Wisconsin/Minnesota border. It follows the Wisconsin portion of the route designated as the Lake Superior Circle Tour, which traverses three states and Canada. If a traveler enters Wisconsin from its western border or comes up from southern Wisconsin the book lends itself to either route since it highlights the recommended stops in the towns regardless of the direction traveled.

The major highways comprising the route along Wisconsin's northern shore are US 2, one of the oldest federal highways in the United States and Wisconsin State Highway 13. The western segment of US 2 begins at Ignace, Michigan, at the foot of the northern terminus of the Mackinaw Bridge and proceeds west across the United States 2,112 miles, crossing seven states before ending at Everett, Washington. The distance within Wisconsin, between Ironwood, Michigan and Duluth, Minnesota is 108 miles. Wisconsin State Highway 13 begins just south of the Wisconsin Dells and proceeds north to Ashland, Wisconsin, heads west with US 2 for approximately four miles and then leaves US 2 circling the Bayfield peninsula before heading west along the lake shore to a point just east of Superior, Wisconsin, where it terminates at its second junction with US 2, for a total distance of 375 miles. The distance between Ashland and Superior via ST 13 is 104 miles.

Both highways traverse scenic parts of the north woods, since substantial portions of the Chequamegon-Nicolet National Forest are included on their paths. Other portions of the route are sparsely populated, allowing the traveler to enjoy the forested views and wildflowers along the way. Wild animals, especially deer, are common sights. Black bears, foxes, wolves and coyotes are sometimes seen ambling across the road as are lines of wild turkeys. Be especially careful when sighting deer since it is not uncommon for them to dart out into the highway when least expected—especially at dawn and dusk. Slow down, beep your horn and flash your lights if a deer is standing on or near the road—and be aware that deer seldom travel alone.

In addition to the recommended stops along the way, historical information is provided to make your trip more informative and interesting. Appendices at the rear of the book contain additional historical information about the area, including its connection with President Kennedy. Since it is unlikely you will be able to stop at all the recommended places during your initial trip to this beautiful area you should plan to make additional trips to immerse yourself thoroughly in this north woods experience on the shore of the world's largest fresh water lake. You won't regret it.

So let's get started . . . .

WISCONSIN'S
LAKE SUPERIOR SHORE

THE APOSTLE ISLANDS

RED CLIFF

ST 13

CORNUCOPIA

HERBSTER

PORT WING

BAYFIELD

MADELINE ISLAND
LA POINTE

LAKE
SUPERIOR

SUPERIOR

WASHBURN

CHEQUAMEGON BAY

MINNESOTA

POPLAR

US 2

BRULE

IRON RIVER

ODANAH

ASHLAND

US 2

HURLEY

MICHIGAN

ST 13

From The Michigan Border to Ashland

After crossing into Wisconsin on US 2 at the Michigan border, the first town encountered just south of the highway is Hurley, population approximately 1500, a somewhat sleepy town today, a far cry from its wilder days from the mid-19th century to the early 20th century, when saloons and houses of ill repute were its principal businesses. It served the lumberjacks and miners who worked in the area. In all probability its most famous visitor was Senator John F. Kennedy, who briefly stopped there on March 17, 1960, as part of his trip through northern Wisconsin during the presidential primary season. He had come up State Highway 13 to Mellen and then diverted to Hurley, before continuing on to Ashland on US 2.

About ten miles west of the Michigan border on the north side of the road is a scenic outlook on a hill where, on a clear day, you can get your first look of the shining blue water of Lake Superior, far on the horizon, over the overgrown brush.

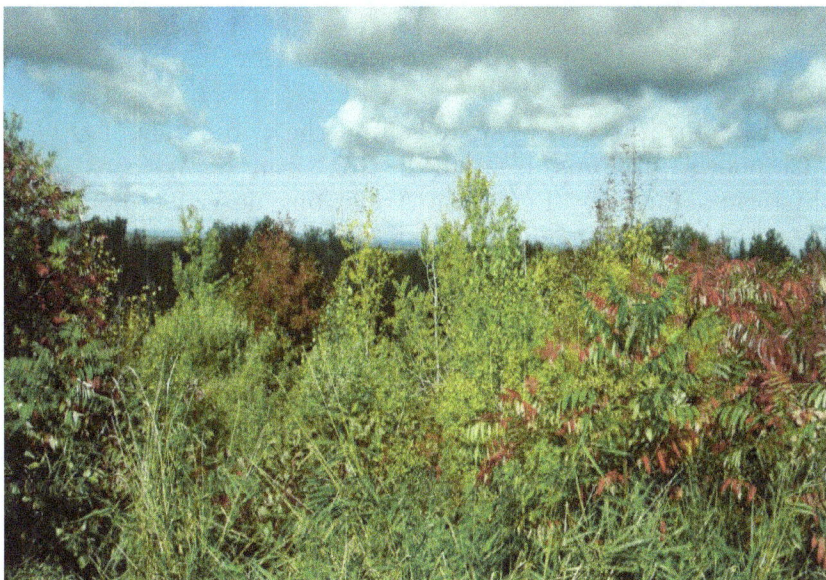

A glimpse of Lake Superior, on the horizon.

Approximately six miles east of Ashland is the town of Odanah, on the Bad River Indian Reservation. The biggest attraction here, located on US 2, is the Bad River Indian Casino and Convention Center.

Casino and Convention Center

There is an interesting story behind the two bands of Ojibiwe (Chippewa) Indians located in this area of Wisconsin. A historic account by Benjamin Armstrong describes his trip to Washington, D. C. in 1852, with Chief Buffalo and a party of Ojibwe, enduring many hardships along the way, where they convinced President Millard Fillmore to rescind the U. S. government order to remove the Ojibwe from their historic homeland in the Apostle Islands area. One band, under the guidance of the Catholic missionaries, settled on the south side of Chequamegon Bay in Odanah, while another band under the guidance of the Protestant missionaries settled north of Bayfield in Red Cliff. The reference to obtain the story of the trip to Washington can be found under "Native American History" in the information sources section.

6

Ashland—Lake Superior's Hometown

As you enter the eastern edge of Ashland, population 8216, you will encounter its first major attraction, on the lake side of the road, the AmericInn and Conference Center. The motel has the only water park in Ashland. If space is available, day passes to the pool can be purchased. The motel's rooms on the lake side have a beautiful view of Chequamegon Bay.

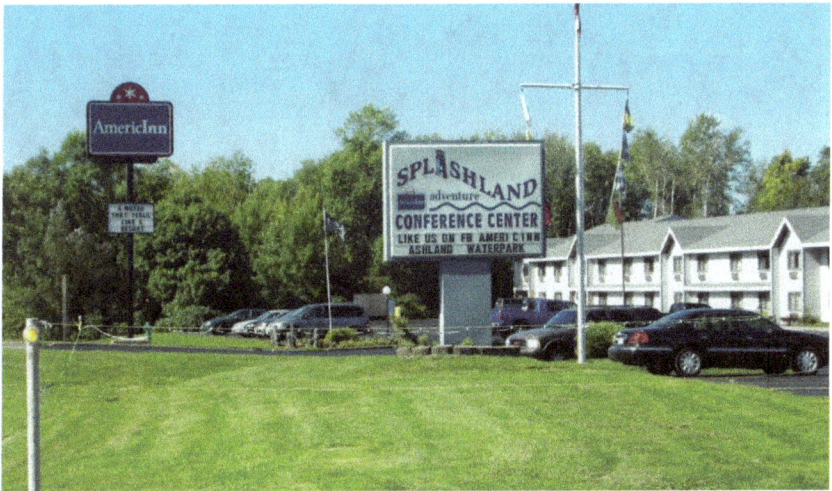

The AmericInn
3009 Lake Shore Drive East
(US 2 is designated as Lake Shore Drive within Ashland)

About 100 yards beyond the AmericInn off Lake Shore Drive is an opportunity to get an expansive view of Chequamegon Bay and a drink of cold artesian water from a deep underground aquifer.

Turn right on 29th Avenue East, a dirt road, and go about fifty yards to a sign announcing the Alan Tomczak Park Public Boat Launch. Turn left and go down the short incline to the boat launching area. To your right will be an artesian well and also a dock. Walk out on the dock to get a view of the broad expanse of Chequamegon Bay and a glimpse of Washburn directly across the bay. When taking a drink of the water, put your hand carefully over the downspout to allow water up through the drinking spigot. If you do it too fast you're going to get splashed. This boat launching area is seldom used due to the shallowness of the water in the boat basin.

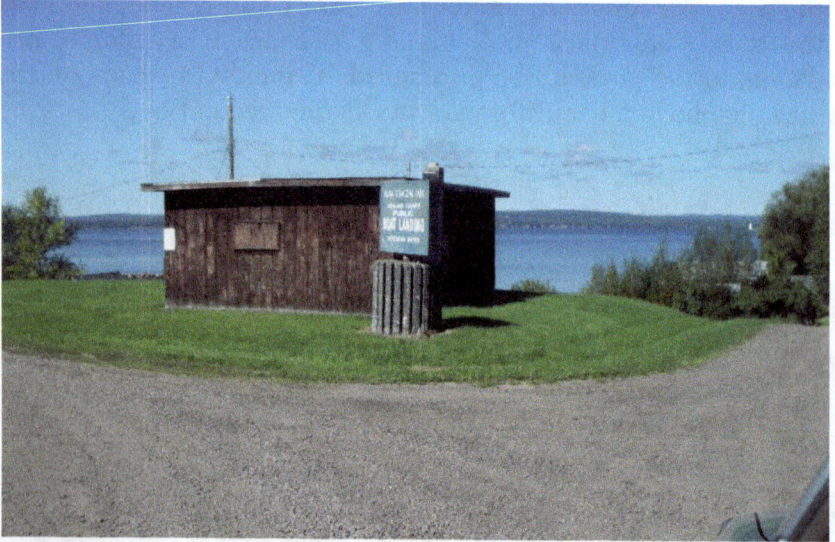

Alan Tomczak Park Public Boat Launch

Artesian Well

Continuing on US 2 about a ½ mile west you will pass in front of a Super Wal-Mart on the south side of the road. On the lake side is the Bayview Motel, formerly the L. Gene Motel. An interesting point about this motel is that a Briton, George Meegan, spent a night here in March 1982, during his successful quest to make the longest recorded walk of 19,019 miles, from the tip of South America (Tierra del Fuego) to the Arctic Ocean off Alaska (January 26, 1977 to September 18, 1983). After he entered the United States at the Mexican border he headed east and passed through Plains, Georgia, where he was granted a meeting with President Jimmy Carter, who signed his travel book. Later in his journey he walked west along the Canadian side of the U. S.-Canadian border and joined US 2 in Michigan. He left US 2 west of Minot, North Dakota, pulling his ever present two wheeled grocery cart, and headed north into Canada. He wrote a book describing his journey aptly titled *The Longest Walk*.

Along this stretch you will see underwater wood pilings remaining from the old Northwestern ore docks that were taken down in the 1960s. You will also see wood pilings along the shore on the west edge of Ashland representing the remnants of docks that were in heavy use during the city's industrial era in the late nineteenth and early twentieth century.

As you proceed west past the Bayview Motel you will pass some open coast line just past a car dealership on the lake side. From this view you can get a look at the Chequamegon Bay lighthouse, over 100 years old, in the distance, which is at the west end of a long breakwater that protects the Ashland coastline from northeast winds. This structure is one of the few remaining examples of lighthouses made of poured concrete. Unfortunately, although the advantage of a breakwater is evident there have been instances of power boats slamming into the breakwater at night, due to ignorance or inattention of the boat's captain.

Chequamegon Bay Lighthouse and Breakwater

An historic information sign on the lake side of the road in this area honors Fleet Admiral William D. Leahy, who was raised in Ashland.   Admiral Leahy was President Franklin D. Roosevelt's military chief of staff during World War II. He can be seen in many of the photographs that were taken at the historic conferences held during the war with Winston Churchill of Great Britain and Joseph Stalin of the Soviet Union.

A large portrait of William Leahy in full military dress is located on the lower level of the   Hotel Chequamegon. There are probably a lot of people who have looked at that portrait and asked themselves, "Who's he?", little realizing the historic events in which he participated. Ashland held a "Welcome Home" parade for Leahy in 1948.

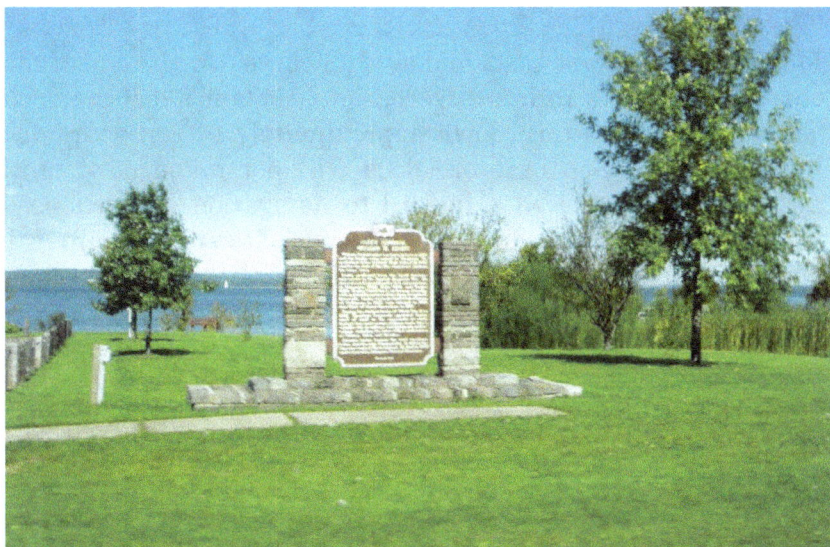
Historic sign honoring Fleet Admiral Leahy

Just up the road on the lake side is Frankie's Pizza, which makes the best thin crust Chicago style pizza in town (my personal view). Frankie's had a large 50th anniversary celebration that spilled over into the parking lot in 2013.

Frankie's Pizza

Moving further west US 2 makes an S curve. At the end of this curve used to be a railroad overpass to Ashland's last ore dock. The overpass was torn down approximately fifteen years ago, but the former Soo Line ore dock was not taken down until 2013, being considered a hazard to navigation as portions of the dock were falling into the lake. A citizens committee is developing plans for the recreational use of the ore dock base which was not removed.

Ashland's Last Ore Dock Before Demolition

Ashland was the hub of the region's industrial activity that began in the mid-nineteenth century and continued into the 20th. At one time it had five ore docks loading huge ships, some more than two football fields in length, that carried iron ore to the industrial Midwest steel mills. The last ore shipment left Ashland in 1965, shortly after the availability of high grade iron ore in the area declined.

Continuing west about a ½ mile, US 2 joins Wisconsin State Highway 13 coming up from the south. A stoplight marks this intersection. To your left is the majestic Hotel Chequamegon, located on the lakefront, next to the city's band shell. It was constructed in a style reminiscent of a former hotel of the same name that stood across the street back in the late nineteenth century. The lobby and sitting room have a distinctive late nineteenth century ambience. The hotel has a restaurant and bar located downstairs, Molly Cooper's, which has a large outdoor porch overlooking the marina and Chequamegon Bay where, when weather permits, meals and drinks are served. From this vantage point a diner has one of the best views available of the sun setting over the Bayfield hills. Be sure to read the history of the bar's name.

The Hotel Chequamegon

Just west of the hotel is the city's band shell where various ceremonies are held during the year beginning with the Memorial Day observance.

13

The Ashland Band Shell

If you turn south at the light at the intersection of US 2 and State Route 13 in front of the Hotel Chequamegon and go south on Ellis Avenue one block you will come to Main Street. Turn right and go down the street observing the landmarks on Ashland's principal retail thoroughfare.

On your right, one block up Main Street, is the Ashland County Courthouse. The courthouse was built early in the 20th century and has large cavernous halls housing the various county departments. Just inside the front entrance is a collection of stuffed animals that are indigenous to the area.

Be sure to read the reference to the courthouse in the Kennedy connection section at the rear of this book.

The Ashland County Courthouse

Throughout Ashland you will observe murals painted on the sides of buildings depicting the history of the area. One of the first you will see as you pass the courthouse is located on the east side of the store on the northwest corner of Main and 3rd Avenue West. It is one of the newest murals, painted shortly before the last ore dock on the Ashland waterfront was taken down in 2013. The ore dock had been scheduled to be taken down in 2012 but a pair of peregrine falcons made their nest on the structure that year, postponing the planned dismantling of the dock.

Ashland has been designated the Historic Mural Capital of Wisconsin. A brochure describing the city's many murals and their locations is available at the Ashland Chamber of Commerce (1716 Lake Shore Drive West) or the Ashland Museum (216 Main Street West). New murals are added almost yearly, so it's possible you may see one being painted by the artists Kelly Meredith and Susan Martinsen, as you make your tour of the downtown area.

Ore Dock Mural

Storefronts Mural

Located off the south side of Main Street on the southeast corner of Fourth Avenue West is another excellent mural, depicting the stores of an earlier era.

The Soo Line Depot, located a couple blocks south of Main Street at 400 3rd Avenue West, is an outstanding example of brownstone construction On April 1, 2000, some years after the depot was first refurbished, it sustained extensive fire damage. It was reconstructed at a cost of 2 ½ million dollars.

The Soo Line Depot

In front of the Soo Line Depot under a protective structure is a decapod locomotive 950 built in 1900, the only 10-wheel drive coal locomotive ever built.

Soo Line Locomotive Decapod 950
Directly across from the Soo Line Depot

Ashland's downtown area has been revitalized with many new boutique shops. However, there are still some structures in the area that evoke memories of the past, including the Bay Theatre (built in 1937), the Vaughn library, (established in 1886), and the Huhn's drug store located in a former Masonic Lodge facility. Visit the New England Store if you have a chance, which has an interesting assortment of items.

The distinctive building with the high steeple located on the northwest corner of Main Street and 6th Avenue West, is the Ashland City Hall. This building is another fine example of brownstone construction. Pedestrians can enter into a nearby tunnel that leads to a scenic view of Chequamegon Bay.

A block past the city hall is Chapple Avenue. If you turn south off Main Street you will find one of Ashland's finest coffee shops—The Black Cat. Across the street is a bakery making specialty breads and other baked goods—Ashland Baking Company. A farmer's market is held in this area on Saturday mornings during the summer months.

The Bay Theater
420 Main Street West

The Vaughn Public Library
502 Main Street West

Huhn Drug Store
522 W. Main Street

New England Store
518 W Main Street

Ashland City Hall
601 Main Street West

Entrance to Tunnel Under Lake Shore Drive

Black Cat Coffee Shop
211 Chapple Avenue

Ashland Baking Company
212 Chapple Avenue

If you continue further west on Main Street you will come to the Deep Water Grille, one of Ashland's finest restaurants, and the adjoining South Shore Brewery.

The Deep Water Grille
808 Main Street West

For those interested in obtaining further information about the area, including free brochures, be sure to visit the Ashland Chamber of Commerce and the Ashland Historical Museum. The personnel at both places are always pleasant and ready to answer any of your questions. The Ashland Chamber sponsors an annual Chequamegon Bay Birding and Nature Festival in mid-May that draws "birders" from across the nation. See the reference section for further information.

A bit of information regarding the color of the water in Chequamegon Bay. . . The majority of the time it is a beautiful blue on sunny days—however if there have been recent heavy rains or very windy days the water takes on a distinctive reddish color due to the mud that is stirred up from the shallow bottom of the bay. This color is due to the abundance of iron in the soil and the "rust" that oxygen produces.

23

Ashland Chamber of Commerce
1716 Lake Shore Drive West

Ashland Historical Museum
216 Main Street West

If you have the time be sure to take a drive through the historical residential area of Ashland where you will be able to see the "gingerbread" houses. These houses are found south of Main Street on Vaughn, Chapple and MacArthur Avenues. More are found on the west side of 2nd Avenue East. Examples of these houses are shown on the following pages.

West side of 2nd Avenue East

Heading west out of Ashland on Lake Shore Drive (US 2/ST 13) you will pass the River Rock Lodge and Bait Shop, an excellent place to find out where the fish are biting in the area.

River Rock Inn and Bait Ship
1200 Lake Shore Drive West

El Dorado, an excellent Mexican restaurant, will be found further west and an historic restaurant, The Platter, currently between owners, is located one block south of the highway. There is a sign on the south side of the highway, pointing the way. The restaurant is located in an historic brownstone building, which once was a house of ill repute for the upper class of the area in the late nineteenth century. Presidential candidate John F. Kennedy had dinner here during one of his trips to the area during the Wisconsin primary season of 1960.

El Dorado Restaurant
2320 Lake Shore Drive West

The Platter Restaurant
315 Turner Road

There are two artesian wells on the west end of Ashland. One is located off the same road that leads to The Platter Restaurant in Prentice Park, which also has a large pond where many ducks, and sometimes swans, can be found. The other artesian well is located at Maslowski Beach on the lake front just a short distance up Highway 2.

From Ashland to Washburn

Heading west out of Ashland you will come to a roundabout where US 2 and State Highway 13 diverge. US 2 continues due west towards Superior, Wisconsin, while State Highway 13 heads northeast along the Chequamegon Bay and Lake Superior shore.

Approximately a ¼ mile west on US 2 you will come to County Highway G, which leads to the entrance of the Northern Great Lakes Visitor Center. A stop here is highly recommended. There is no entrance fee and the exhibits within the center are very interesting and informative. The gift shop within the center, Spirit of the North, has a wide variety of books and souvenirs. After visiting the center return towards the roundabout and follow State Highway 13 to Washburn and Bayfield.

Entrance to the Great Lakes Visitor Center

About 2-½ miles up ST 13 you will come to Barksdale, an unincorporated town consisting of a handful of houses on the lake side of ST 13, directly across from the former 1,800 acre Du Pont explosives manufacturing facility which opened in 1904 and closed in 1971. At one time it employed over 6,000 workers and was the largest explosives manufacturing facility in the United States. It manufactured many thousands of tons of explosives that were used in the area for land clearance and mining. During World Wars I and II and the Korean War it also supplied explosive propellants used in the manufacture of military ammunition. It was a huge operation and had several train tracks upon its property. As might be expected it had some accidents including one major one in October 1952 that killed eight men. The explosive force from this accident broke many windows in Ashland. A large model of the facility can be found in the Washburn Cultural Center. The original entrance to the facility, consisting of mortared stone columns with a steel gate, still stands and can be seen on the north side of the highway just before entering the west side of Barksdale.

Former entrance to Du Pont manufacturing facility

A few miles further down on the west side of the road is the studio of a famous wood carver of the area, William P. Vienneaux. His specialty is carving figures from logs using a hand-held chain saw. His studio is adjacent to a closed bait shop, formerly Northern Allure. His roadside studio is easy to miss since it is hidden by tall bushes and trees. His sculptures, which include totem poles, can be seen in the Chequamegon Bay area and have been shipped throughout the world. He recently underwent open heart surgery but appears to be back at work, strong as ever.

The Wayward Wind outdoor studio of Wm. Vienneaux

Washburn—A Small Town
On The Greatest Lake

As the highway enters Washburn, population 2117, around a sweeping curve to the right you will shortly come to one of the nicest coffee/latte cafes in the area on the north side of the road—North Coast Coffee. If the weather allows you can sit outside and enjoy the atmosphere of this town and do a little people watching. State Highway 13 is designated as Bayfield Street within Washburn.

The North Coast Coffee Shop
509 West Bayfield Street

A few blocks up the street, on the lake side, is a long-established crafts shop selling paintings, sculptures and art related supplies, Karlyn's Gallery. The previous owner, Karlyn Holman, who passed away in 2020, was an accomplished artist and world traveler, attending art tours and classes throughout Europe. Originals and copies of her artwork are available for sale at the shop

Karlyn's Gallery
318 W. Bayfield Street

Adjacent to Karlyn's you will find Da Lou's Bistro, where wood-fired pizzas are its specialty during the evening hours.

DaLou's Bistro
310 W. Bayfield St.

Further up the street you will come to Coco's, a busy café and bakery. Coco's has an extensive assortment of made-to-order sandwiches, delicious soups and bakery items plus a very friendly and efficient staff. Lunchtime waits can sometimes be long but the food is well worth it. They also carry an extensive selection of gluten-free items. If weather permits you can take a seat at one of the outside tables.

Coco's Café and Bakery
146 W. Bayfield Street

Further down the street take a right turn and drive down to the lake for a beautiful view of Chequamegon Bay from the Washburn Marina. You can see the twinkling lights of Ashland across the bay after it turns dark. The former restaurant near the marina is now used for special events.

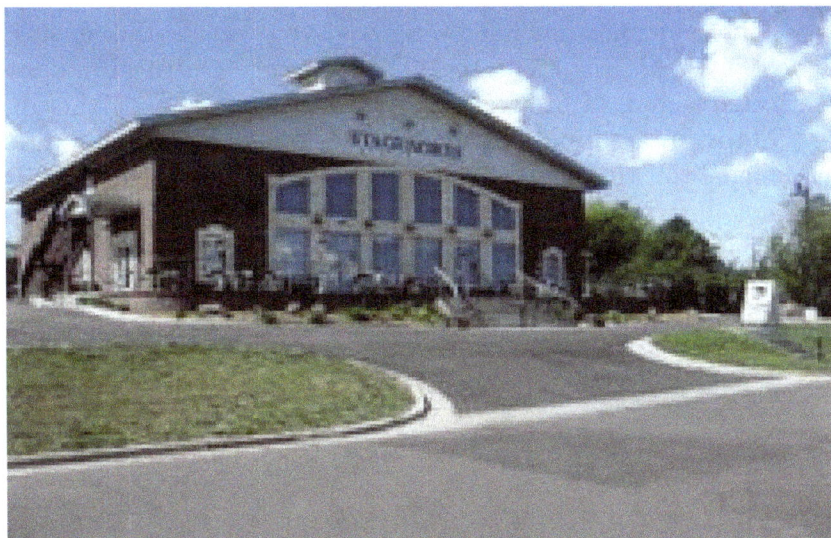

The Stage North
123 E. Omaha Street

On the left side of the road to the marina is the Stage North theatre and bar, which presents a variety of live entertainment throughout the year, including the Big Water film festival in mid-November.

The Washburn Marina

The last recommended stop as you reach the east end of Washburn is the Washburn Cultural Center, constructed of brownstone, on the west side of the road. Many interesting exhibits can be found here, including the model of the Du Pont explosives manufacturing facility, noted earlier. Among the other exhibits are detailed histories of the town's founding families.

Washburn Cultural Center
1 E. Bayfield St.

From Washburn to Bayfield

About 1-½ miles north of Washburn is Houghton Falls Road that leads to a ¼ mile trail that follows the edge of a scenic forested canyon to the water's edge. The public parking area is located approximately a ¼ mile before the road ends.

A lake view at the end of the Houghton Falls trail

If you make your trip in mid to late June you will see the wild lupine flowers in bloom (pronounced lu-pin). They are found growing profusely between Bayfield and Washburn along Highway 13 and along the orchard roads west of Bayfield. Although there have been many attempts to plant lupines in other areas south of Washburn, they have mostly been unsuccessful, apparently because of differences in soil conditions.

Lupines in bloom

The road to Big Top Chautauqua is located about three miles south of Bayfield, off Highway 13 (Ski Hill Road). There is a small carnival wagon on the northwest corner of the junction with Highway 13. Various musical attractions are presented during summer evenings. Among the talented performers who have performed here are Johnny Cash and Willie Nelson. If possible, see the performance of "Riding The Wind", an excellent musical exposition of Bayfield and the Apostle Islands. A list of the current attractions can be found in the Chamber of Commerce office in Bayfield and at their office in Washburn, just south of the Washburn Cultural Center.

Just beyond the road to Big Top Chautauqua is the Bayfield Fish Hatchery, on the west side of the road, which has interesting indoor exhibits, including a large aquarium containing live fish indigenous to the area. The cavernous structure contains a large number of tanks, open to public viewing, containing thousands of fish at various stages of growth.

Bayfield Fish Hatchery Entrance

Approximately three miles south of Bayfield is the Port Superior Marina. The Portside Restaurant is located on the second floor over the Superior Charters office., the major sailboat chartering service in the area. This restaurant has an outstanding view of the Port Superior Marina.

The Portside Restaurant

Port Superior Marina

For those interested in spectacular views of the islands while golfing there is the Apostle Highlands Golf Course, approximately a mile south of Bayfield. The view from the 3rd tee and fairway overlooking the "gap" leading to Lake Superior from Chequamegon Bay between Madeline Island and Long Island is breathtaking.

View from the 3rd tee of the Apostle Highland Golf Course

Just a short distance further south on Highway 13 you can pick up a fresh pie or other freshly baked goods at the Gourmet Garage, a working kitchen and store. You can't miss the large "Pies" sign on the lake side of the road, although it's more easily seen coming south, out of Bayfield.

Just before you enter Bayfield you will come to the Eckel's Pottery Gallery on the west side of the highway. If you're lucky you'll see pottery being made here, as the workshop is adjacent to the showroom.

The Gourmet Garage

Eckel's Pottery

Bayfield—Gateway to the Apostle Islands

Bayfield, founded in 1856, with a current population of approximately 600, strikes one as a New England fishing village in many aspects. The town fathers have, to their credit, not allowed any of the franchise businesses one would normally encounter in other towns and cities. Instead there is a main street (Rittenhouse Avenue) which contains various retail stores and restaurants, having, in most cases, a distinctive retro flavor of a time when life was unhurried and more relaxed—although during the busy holiday periods that feeling can get a little frayed as it becomes crowded. If possible, visit Bayfield outside the holiday periods to appreciate the charm of this town. There are also many bed and breakfast operations in the area. Bayfield was cited as the "Best Little Town in the Midwest" based on an extensive survey conducted by the Chicago Tribune.

Shortly after entering Bayfield from the south ST 13 turns right onto Rittenhouse Avenue. A few blocks after the turn you will see the Rittenhouse Inn on your left at the corner of the intersection with North 3rd St., one of the most famous "bed and breakfast" inns in Wisconsin—if not the country. Managed by Mary and Jerry Phillips for many years, it is now under the capable direction of their daughter, Wendy and her husband. The inn's restaurant, the only "fine dining" restaurant in the area, serves gourmet meals in a Victorian setting. During the summer, outstanding floral arrangements decorate the porch.

The inn is known for its extensive Christmas programs, which include carolers singing during the month of December. Spending a night or two at this famous inn, with its extensive decorations, during the Christmas season is an experience never to be forgotten.

Rittenhouse Inn
301 Rittenhouse Avenue

Located just one block north of Rittenhouse Avenue, on Washington Street, between North 5th St. and North 4th St., is the Apostle Islands National Lakeshore Headquarters. A visit to this facility is encouraged for those wishing to get an initial understanding of the Apostle Islands, the major attraction in this area of Wisconsin. Visitors can view a 20-minute film in a theatre whose showings are available upon request. Spend a little time at the center viewing the exhibits, including a 3rd order beehive Fresnel lens (pronounced Fre-nelle), which was the primary means of focusing the light that went out from the lighthouses in the islands in years past. This particular lens was originally installed in the Michigan Island lighthouse. An interesting point about Fresnel lens, invented in France in the early nineteenth century, is that they are currently used on today's modern aircraft carriers as an aid for pilots bringing their aircraft in for landings.

Staff personnel at the center are very helpful and will answer any questions you have about the Apostle Islands. A diverse selection of free brochures is available, including those describing the more-visited islands, camping, boating, kayaking, and scuba diving. In addition, a wide variety of books on subjects pertinent to the islands are available for purchase. An interesting bit of history regarding the building housing the headquarters is that it served as a German POW facility during 1944-45.

Apostle Islands National Lakeshore Headquarters
415 Washington Avenue

In addition to the many interesting and varied retail shops on Rittenhouse Avenue, the following places, described in the following pages, should be visited, time permitting.

The Chamber of Commerce office, located one block south of Rittenhouse Avenue, on the northeast corner of Manypenny Avenue and Broad St., has many free brochures describing activities in the area—and the personnel are very helpful. Be sure to pick up the free booklet published by Bayfield that contains a map of Bayfield plus information on businesses in the area.

Greunke's Inn located on the northwest corner of Rittenhouse Avenue and North 1st St., has a 40's/50's décor. It was here that John Kennedy, Jr. and his friends spent a night and had breakfast in August 1995, before kayaking in the islands. The restaurant is known for the regional delicacy of whitefish livers.

Bayfield Chamber of Commerce
42 South Broad Street

Greunke's Inn
17 Rittenhouse Avenue

Brownstone Centre, a gift and yarn shop, has an interesting exhibit at the top the stairs going up to the second floor—a large stuffed standing black bear. This bear, while alive, once shared quarters with another black bear on the western edge of Ashland.

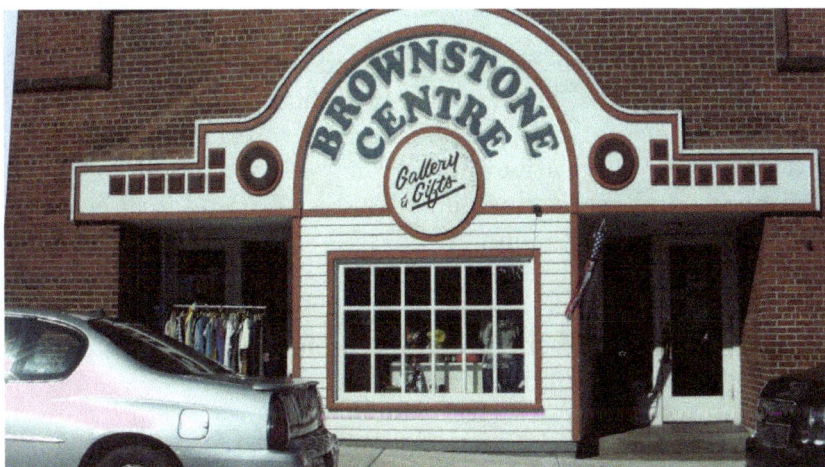

Brownstone Centre
121 Rittenhouse Avenue

The Manypenny Bistro, the former Egg Toss Restaurant, located on Manypenny Avenue, one block south of Rittenhouse Avenue, at the northwest corner of the intersection with South 2nd St., is frequented by many sailors before they depart on their boats into the Apostle Islands.

Manypenny Bistro
41 Manypenny Avenue

Maggie's, a red-hued building, located at the western end of Manypenny Avenue, is open for lunch and dinner. Don't expect a far north décor of moose heads and deer antlers—it's strictly a Caribbean decorative flavor here—with lots of pink flamingos—and the food is delicious. Be prepared for a wait at lunchtime during the summer.

The lakefront area, two blocks south of Rittenhouse Avenue, is the place to obtain freshly caught whitefish or lake trout fillets for dinner. Two fish purveyors are located here.

Maggie's
257 Manypenny Avenue

The Fish House
208 Wilson Avenue

If you're looking for a quiet change of pace, stop in the Honest Dog Books store located just off the northeast corner of the intersection of Manypenny Avenue and South Second St, next to the Stone's Throw gift shop. Used book treasures can be found here. Another fine bookstore is located on the 100 block of Rittenhouse Avenue—Apostle Islands Booksellers

Honest Dog Books and Stone's Throw
38 S. Second Street

Apostle Islands Booksellers
112 Rittenhouse Avenue

There are two museums in the area. The Bayfield Maritime Museum located on the lake front, south of Rittenhouse Avenue, on the northwest corner of Wilson Avenue and South 1st. St., will give you an appreciation for the history of the area and for those who braved the cold waters of Lake Superior. Dave Strzok, the former owner of the cruise service, was the driving force behind the establishment of this museum.

The Bayfield Heritage Association Museum, containing several exhibits covering the history of Bayfield, is located just off the southeast corner of Washington Avenue and North Broad Street.

The Apostle Islands Cruise Service office is located at the foot of Rittenhouse Avenue on the lakefront. They have several cruises scheduled at various times during the week. They also take campers and kayakers to the more popular islands.

The ferry service to Madeline Island is located approximately one block north of Rittenhouse Avenue on the lakeshore. A ferry schedule and a map of the island can be obtained from the ferry office. Vehicles can be transported on the ferry. Most of the captained sailboat tours leave from the city dock. Information regarding these offerings is contained in this book's reference section.

The Keeper of the Light retail store, adjacent to the cruise service ticketing office, has an interesting and extensive collection of nautical and lighthouse merchandise and is the coordinating office for the Lighthouse Celebration cruises held in early September.

Across from the cruise service office on Rittenhouse Avenue is a gazebo that allows travelers to relax and observe the activities on the lake front.

Apostle Islands Cruise Service and Keeper of the Light
2/19 North Front Street

Bayfield Harbor Gazebo

View of the pier at the end of Rittenhouse Avenue

Bayfield Heritage Association Museum
30 N. Broad Street

An extensive area of apple orchards is located west of Bayfield, in the high hills above the town. A map of the orchards can be obtained, at the Bayfield Chamber of Commerce. In addition to the apple crop available in the fall, many of the orchards have fields of strawberries, raspberries and blueberries, some available for public picking throughout the summer months. If visiting during late May or early June be sure to view the orchards when the apple trees are in bloom. Blue Vista Farm and Erickson Orchard are recommended. There is a humorous sign at one of the junctions in the orchard area to the effect that if you are lost let someone else drive.

An historic event concerning Bayfield deserves mention—the Bayfield Flood of '42. A tremendous thunderstorm dumped eight inches of rain during the period July 16-17, 1942, producing a river of water, mud, boulders, coffins and cadavers that washed down from the cemetery in the high hill west of the town. It cascaded through the heart of Bayfield, wiping out many buildings, on its way to the lake. Miraculously, the only casualty was a dog. A prize-winning photographic exhibit of this horrific event is on prominent display in the Bayfield Heritage Association Museum.

And one final note—the most important event on the Bayfield calendar, the Apple Festival, "Applefest", is held on the first weekend in October. This is the highlight of the fall season and the streets of the town are crowded. In addition to several booths of apple related goods there are many others selling everything from soup to nuts—literally. Parking space is at a premium so be prepared for a long walk.

Historic La Pointe On Madeline Island

After a twenty-minute ferry ride from Bayfield you will arrive in La Pointe, the only town on Madeline Island. On your right at the top of the street is the town's post office.

If you continue straight ahead you will come to the Madeline Island Museum, which should be visited to gain an understanding of the rich and varied history of the island, beginning with early Indian settlement and continuing into the 18th century as an important outpost of French exploration and fur trading.

Madeline has 45 miles of paved roads, which allows the visitor to travel throughout the island. La Pointe has a main street containing several commercial establishments, including the Beach Club, which has the best whitefish sandwich in the Apostle Islands area and Tom's Burned Down Café (on Middle Road), which should be visited to experience its uniqueness. Rental mopeds and bicycles are available at the south end of La Pointe's main street. Also located here, near the intersection of Main Street and Middle Road is Adventure Vacations, the major kayak supplier on the island.

Just south of La Pointe is the Madeline Island Yacht Club Marina and the Madeline Island golf course, with as one might expect, spectacular views.

There is an island-studded lagoon, best seen from atop a bluff near the Big Bay Town Park parking area at the north end of Big Bay, considered by many to be the most scenic spot in the islands. Day use of this park and beach is free. Rental canoes and rowboats are available for use in the lagoon. Fishing is allowed (Wisconsin license required)

Big Bay State Park, which occupies a significant part of the middle of the island, has an extensive trail system, 55 camping sites and scenic picnic areas. A brochure, available at the park entrance, contains a map of the park. An entrance fee is required.

Madeline Island Museum
226 Colonel Woods Avenue

Beach Club
817 Fort Road

View from picnic area of Big Bay State Park

View from bluff near Big Bay Town Park

Bridge over lagoon

Kayak entering lagoon outlet to Lake Superior

From Bayfield To Cornucopia

Leaving Bayfield headed north you will encounter Sally's, which is an interesting accumulation of items on both sides of the highway. Although some of the Bayfield residents consider the area an eyesore, others, who are looking for hard to find treasures, such as the blue glass insulators that once graced telephone poles, consider it a collectibles hunter's paradise. It's doubtful a business such as Sally's would be allowed under today's zoning regulations, but the business was grandfathered in due to its long term of existence on the site. Sally herself will usually greet you if you stop except in late July when she sells raspberries she has gathered from her bushes on the southwest corner of Rittenhouse Avenue and Broad Street in Bayfield.

If you come into Bayfield from the north you will have one of the most scenic views of the Bayfield harbor and Madeline Island, just as you pass Sally's.

Sally's Collectibles

Proceeding further north you will enter the Indian reservation town of Red Cliff, where a large casino and resort, Legendary Waters, was recently built. Boaters who desire to risk a few dollars in the casino can usually find a transient space at the Red Cliff Marina, adjacent to the casino.

Legendary Waters Resort and Casino

Home of the Red Cliff Band of Lake Superior Chippewa, Red Cliff is the site of the colorful Tribal Pow-Wow held on the July 4th weekend. For more information go to www.redcliff.org.

Across a short expanse of Lake Superior from Red Cliff (about a mile) you will see the west shore of Basswood Island, one of the twenty-two islands comprising the Apostle Islands National Lakeshore. This area is the closet point to any of the Apostle Islands from the highway.

Basswood Island had extensive brownstone quarrying operations in the late 19th and early 20th centuries. The brownstone used to build the Apostle Islands National Lakeshore Headquarters in Bayfield was taken from this island.

Basswood Island

A few miles up the road on the lake side you will come to County Road K, which will take you to the mainland portion of the Apostle Islands National Lakeshore at Little Sand Bay. A visitor center is located on the grounds near the lake shore. Trails lead from this area along the lake shore.

The remaining fifteen miles to Cornucopia passes through an extensive area of forest far from the lake shore, with no views of the lake. However, if you make this drive in mid to late September you will see a brilliant display of autumn colors. Another area with an excellent fall colors is the stretch of Highway 2 that goes directly from Ashland to Superior,

During the winter, if conditions are right, park visitors can enter the lake shore's sea caves from a trail accessed at Myers Beach, a few miles north of Cornucopia. Spectacular photos of the interior of the caves in the winter of 2013-2014 with their countless numbers of frozen giant icicles were shown in newspapers nationally. Be sure to call the park service before attempting a trip to the sea caves to determine if visits are being allowed.

Northern Wisconsin's fall colors

Another view of the fall colors

Cornucopia

Approaching Cornucopia, population about 100, you will have a beautiful view of the lake. One of the prettiest beaches on the northern shore of Lake Superior is found in this small town—Siskiwit Bay beach. The beach has no protection from winds coming from the north across the great expanse of Lake Superior so be prepared for spectacular incoming waves during windy days.

Home of Wisconsin's northernmost post office, this small fishing community has a marina, a general store and a large community building, which is the site of the region's best fish fry, an all-you-can-eat affair, held on the first Sunday in July. Many of the town's citizens participate in this annual event, including youngsters who circulate among the long community style tables with plates of extra fish. It's a simple set fare meal of deep fried whitefish, homemade potato salad, bread, butter, green onions and radishes. Coffee and lemonade are also served. Get there early if you want to avoid the long lines that start forming at 10:00 AM.

Another well-attended town event is Corny Day, held on the second Saturday in August, drawing visitors from miles around. A long line of patrons for the delicious freshly made whitefish sandwiches usually starts forming before noon.

Be sure to stop by the Green Shed Museum near the harbor, which contains many artifacts from the past, giving the visitor a better understanding of the history of the area.

Ehler's general store has an extensive assortment of varied merchandise, being one of the few stores on this sparsely populated shore of Lake Superior. One gets the feeling this type of store was the norm in the early days of settlement throughout the United States.

Town of Bell Community Center
Site of the Annual Cornucopia Fish Fry

Ehler's General Store

Just across from Ehler's about fifty yards towards the lake, is Corny Coffee and Sweet Shop, which as the name implies offers made to order coffee and an assortment of pastries.

Corny Coffee And Sweet Shop
88610 Superior Avenue

Just west of Siskiwit Beach, off the highway, is a group of buildings housing various retail stores including The Good Earth Shop, which has a variety of retail offerings

The Good Earth Shop
22670 Siskiwit Bay Parkway

Cornucopia to the Minnesota Border

The drive from Cornucopia to its junction with Highway 2, just east of the city of Superior, passes through two small towns, Herbster and Port Wing.

Herbster, population 104, approximately eight miles west of Cornucopia, has a beautiful campground on Lake Superior's shore and a few retail shops.

Port Wing, population 164, is approximately seven miles west of Herbster. It has the last harbor on Lake Superior's southern shore before reaching the city of Superior, another fifteen miles to the west. The biggest event in the town is the Annual Fish Boil of lake trout, held on the Saturday of Labor Day weekend—as they say, rain or shine.

For those wishing to try something entirely different from a culinary standpoint, make the trek up to Port Wing on the second Saturday in December for a lutefisk dinner, a Nordic staple that almost nobody likes. Lutefisk traces its origins back to a time in Scandinavia when the preservation of fish was necessary for long periods, using a method that produced a food which was unpalatable to wild animals. Fish are soaked in lye and then dried for a long period. When preserved they look like white planks of wood. The best method of reconstituting the mummified fish for the dinner table, after thoroughly rinsing the lye out with water, is to soak it in milk and steam it, giving it a jelly-like consistency—and a strong fishy odor. Bon appétit!

If you have a little more time and wish to take a more scenic route to Superior you can take County Road C, east from Cornucopia back to Washburn, and then turn south to Ashland, where you hook up with US 2.

Headed west on US 2 from Ashland you will pass through Iron River, Brule and Poplar.

For those looking for a thoroughly unique breakfast or lunch dining experience be sure to stop in at the Delta Diner, in Delta, Wisconsin. It's a short trip south of Highway 2, about 12 miles west of the roundabout on the west edge of Ashland. Turn south on County Highway E and go about 3 miles to County Highway H, where you turn right. The Delta Diner is about 6 miles down the road on the left side. See the reference section for its web address and phone number for hours.

Delta Diner
14385 County Highway H

When passing through Iron River, stop at the Rustic Roost if you're hungry. Their turkey dinners can't be beat.

Further down US 2 you'll come to the town of Brule and the Bois Brule River, a favorite of canoeists, nicknamed the River of the Presidents, since several presidents have stayed at the Cedar Lodge, an exclusive lodging facility on the river that caters to fishermen. The river is noted for its rainbow trout. Canoes can be rented in Brule and transport to put-in points on the river are provided.

In 1928 President Calvin Coolidge spent a good portion of the summer at the Cedar Lodge. It's interesting to note that in the 1920s a president could leave the sweltering humidity of Washington, D. C. to spend most of the summer in a remote part of northern Wisconsin, far from the nation's capital, and long before there were instant forms of communication. Coolidge obviously took his campaign slogan of 1924 to heart—"Keep Cool With Coolidge." Will Rogers, a well-known humorist of the time, put Coolidge's attitude towards his job succinctly when he said, "He is the first president to discover that what the American people want is to be left alone."

The tiny town of Poplar would probably have been unmentioned and forgotten, except for a boy who grew up here—Richard Bong. He became America's #1 ace of World War II, shooting down over 40 airplanes, and was awarded the Congressional Medal of Honor by General Douglas MacArthur. He died as a test pilot in 1945 at age 24 and is buried in Poplar. His death was page one news, sharing space with the announcement of the atomic bombing of Hiroshima. A museum highlighting his achievements and those of other airmen will be seen as you enter Superior, the last Wisconsin city before you cross a large expanse of water, a confluence of several rivers, flowing into Lake Superior. Duluth, Minnesota, is on the other side of the bridge.

Major Richard Bong

69

APPENDIX I

LAKE SUPERIOR FACTS

- Lake Superior contains 10% of all the fresh water on earth, and more than all the other Great Lakes combined— 3,000,000,000,000,000   (3 quadrillion) gallons.

- It is the largest fresh water lake in the world based on surface area—31,700 square miles. Lake Baikal in Russia is larger based on volume, being much deeper. It holds over twice the amount of water as Lake Superior.

- The lake rarely freezes over completely. Complete freezing occurred in 1962, 1979, 2003, 2009 and 2014.

- The average depth of the lake is 483 feet, with the deepest point north of Marquette, Michigan—1,333 feet. Lake Baikal's deepest point is 5,387 feet.

- Lake Superior is considered the earth's youngest major feature, formed a mere 10,000 years ago, following the melting of the last glacier. Lake Baikal was formed 25 million years ago.

- There are 78 different species of fish found in the lake.

- The average underwater visibility in the lake is 27 feet, making it the cleanest and clearest of the Great Lakes.

- The largest wave ever recorded on Lake Superior was 31 feet high. Waves of 20 feet occur regularly each year during storms.

- There have been about 350 shipwrecks recorded in Lake Superior.

- Lake Superior is 25 feet higher than Lake Huron into which it drains at the rapids of Sault Ste. Marie, Michigan. Locks at this point allow ships to enter Lake Superior or the St. Mary's River, which leads to Lake Huron.

- The lake is 350 miles long and 160 miles wide at its widest point. It is fed by over 200 rivers.

- Although the temperature of the surface water varies seasonally, swimming in the lake even during the summer can result in hypothermia, since the water temperature is usually around 50 degrees at that time.

- One of the strangest stories of survival on Lake Superior concerns a boat crewman, 28-year old Scott Richards, who fell off an ore boat, 40 feet into the lake, at 3:00 AM on October 11, 1999, as it was rounding Michigan's Keweenaw Peninsula. As luck would have it the air temperature and the water were comparatively mild for that time of year, and the wind was blowing towards the shore. Scott was also a strong swimmer, with a will to survive, and swam the five miles to shore. The retired couple who let the soaked and bedraggled Richards into their home at Eagle Harbor called the sheriff who found Scott's story incredulous—the first time anyone had been known to survive such an experience.

APPENDIX II
HISTORY OF THE AREA

Much of Wisconsin's northern shore and Lake Superior were sculpted from 600 million year old sandstone by a series of glaciers that arrived around 2-½ million years ago and receded in the final period of glaciation about 10,000 years ago. Most of the beautiful stones found along the shores of the beaches in the area were carried by the glaciers hundreds of miles and dropped as they melted. It's hard to imagine the immense power of these rivers of ice, which were over a mile high. The weight of the glaciers caused the ice at its bottom to become pliable and flow south inexorably, gouging the earth as it went. The northeast shore of Lake Superior is still rebounding from the weight of the last glacier at the rate of almost two feet per century.

Initially, as the last glacier melted, the level of Lake Superior was hundreds of feet higher and only portions of two of the Apostle Islands were above water—Bear and Oak. Ancient beachlines can be found on both these islands. Later, about the time the pyramids were being built, the lake began dropping to its current level, uncovering the remaining islands. At some point Superior's waters began flowing towards the other Great Lakes in the vicinity of Sault Ste. Marie at Lake Superior's eastern end. One can only imagine the deluge of water that cascaded into the area, now known as the St. Mary's River, on its way to Lake Huron and Lake Michigan.

The early years of the 21st century have shown some substantial variation in Lake Superior's level, which is dependent, in great part, on precipitation throughout the year. The lake's level dropped almost 1-½ feet in 2007, a level not seen since the early 20th century. This drop caused some important changes in the shorelines, dock usability and water flows into bog areas. However, the lake's level recovered to its earlier level in the years that followed.

The history of early human habitation has been difficult to document, although there is some evidence dating back five thousand years that humans inhabited the area, sometime after the glaciers receded. More recently, Native American oral histories indicate that the Ojibwe (Chippewa) migrated from the east to the area about the time that Christopher Columbus sailed for the New World. Other Indian tribes were also active in the area including the Sioux, Huron, Fox and Ottawa.

Some 150 years later, around the time the Pilgrims were landing on Plymouth Rock, French explorers were making their way into the far reaches of Lake Superior. In 1659, two French trappers, Radisson and Grosilliers, established a camp at the southwest corner of Chequamegon Bay, west of present day Ashland. During an active exploratory period French voyageurs established trade routes for their fur trading activities along the Great Lakes, including a portage route through the Bois Brule River to connect with the Mississippi River. The French lost control to the British in 1762 after the French and Indian War. Subsequently, the area became part of the United States after the War of 1812. The region was designated as part of the Michigan Territory in 1818, redesignated as part of the Wisconsin Territory in 1836, and eventually included in the state in 1848.

Following a comparatively quiet period, the area was involved in extensive development of its natural resources. This development was aided by immigrants from Northern Europe, beginning in the mid-1800s, close on the heels of the opening of the Sault Ste. Marie locks at the eastern end of Lake Superior and the arrival of the railroad. In addition to the significant commercial fishing in the area, there was intensive lumbering in the islands and the surrounding mainland. In the winter of 1892-3 there were approximately 10,000 men employed in harvesting timber in the area. Lumber mills sprang up in the Bayfield area and along Chequamegon Bay. At the height of the lumbering activity, Ashland alone had eight sawmills running around the clock. The quarrying of high quality brownstone from the islands and the mainland provided building material for many of the large Midwestern cities. A prime example of this construction can be found in the building, formerly a courthouse, housing the Apostle Islands National Lakeshore Headquarters in Bayfield.

The shipment of iron ore bound for Midwest steel mills from mines near Ashland was an enormous undertaking. Long trains carried ore to several docks in Ashland where it was loaded onto huge ore carriers, some almost two football fields in length. There were over twenty active mines supplying ore to the Ashland docks in 1892. The Du Pont Corporation built the largest explosives production facilities in the United States on Chequamegon Bay, providing significant quantities of the explosives for munitions used in both World Wars and for land clearance, mining and quarrying in the area. Ashland also was a major distribution point for coal mined in the eastern United States. In May 1893 shipments of freight from the Chequamegon Bay area exceeded four million tons. Daily train arrivals and departures during that period averaged 385—both freight and passenger. Even with the bustling commercial activity in the region tourists came to the islands to escape the heat in the Midwestern cities and to view the area's raw beauty.

During the mid-1890s the Chequamegon Bay region was the second busiest shipping area in the western Great Lakes, surpassed only by Chicago. It shipped nearly twice the tonnage of Milwaukee, Duluth and Superior combined. One can get a feeling for the volume of shipping activity through the Apostle Islands during this commercial period based on one hour's count of 105 ships passing by the Devils Island lighthouse. If one could compare the horns, whistles, dynamite blasts, whining saws of the numerous lumber mills, the steam hammering in the quarries and the chugging of steam locomotives hauling their loads of iron ore of this period with the serenity experienced today, the contrast would be stark. The commercial boom of this period ended very quickly.

By the mid-20th century, the commercial fishing industry had collapsed due to overfishing and the depredation of the sea lamprey brought about by the construction of the Welland Canal around Niagara Falls. Brownstone quarrying ended much earlier due to new construction methods involving steel. Today's overgrown quarry sites in the area contain brownstone blocks ready for shipping that lay were they were on the last working day. It's as if someone just blew a whistle and said, "It's all over, boys!" The quality of the iron ore taken from the Gogebic Range, east of Ashland, was no longer economically viable for iron production, resulting in the closing of the mines and the Ashland ore docks. Subsequently, the railroads that had carried the ore discontinued all service into the area. The large stands of lumber were gone and lumbering operations moved on to other areas to the north and west. The TNT plant drastically phased down operations after World War II and finally closed. Open pit mining in the west eliminated the need for eastern coal distribution through Ashland. In a comparatively short number of years the area became what it is today. Only the tourists kept coming—and in greater numbers.

Time is a great healer and today the area is once again heavily forested. In only sixty years, the time since most of the last lumbering took place, the white pine, the colossus of the northern forests, is beginning to show its future dominance as it breaks through the forest canopies. The cacophony of the earlier period of commercial activity has given way to the timeless sounds of waves lapping on sandy beaches and rocky shorelines, innumerable bird calls and the rustling of wind-driven leaves in the forest canopy. Today the area is a veritable paradise for hikers, campers, and boaters of all types. The term "rewilding" has been given to the process of the forest regenerating itself and healing its wounds.

76

Since Lake Superior is the largest freshwater lake in the world based on area, its power is immense. It can create its own weather, and storms can be devastating. There have been many ships lost in the vicinity of the Apostle Islands, most prior to accurate weather forecasting. But even in comparatively recent times, large ships have gone down in Lake Superior's waters as evidenced by the fate of the ore carrier *Edmund Fitzgerald* in November 1975. The lighthouses sprinkled throughout the Apostle Islands were built in the late 1800s to assist the ships entering or passing by the islands. The islands also have been a place of refuge for the large lake ships transiting the length of Lake Superior. During most of the 20th century, it was not unusual for large ships to be seen at anchor in the safety of the islands waiting out lake storms.

The road that led to the Apostle Islands becoming a National Lakeshore is an interesting one. The first attempt to have the islands declared a national treasure ended badly. In 1930, Congress ordered a report be made on a proposal for the Apostle Islands National Park. The inspector who was sent in accordance with Congress's request, Harlan Kelsey, a Boston landscape architect, was certainly not impressed with what he saw. The islands had just been stripped of their trees and had suffered extensive fire damage. It must have looked like a scene from a World War I battlefield rather than as a venue for a national park. Shortly after his trip, he issued a report throwing cold water on the proposal.

Some thirty years later interest in giving the islands a national park designation arose again. Unfortunately, the assassination of President Kennedy, a potential supporter of the cause and the turmoil and escalating costs of the Vietnam War, put these efforts on hold. Budget constraints had an impact on the size of the park as originally envisioned, and planned amenities, such as a scenic highway along the Bayfield peninsula. Senate hearings were finally held in 1967 and 1969, culminating in the passage of Public Law 91-424 by Congress in late 1970, providing for the establishment of the Apostle Islands National Lakeshore. President Nixon signed the bill into law on September 26, 1970.

Following the national lakeshore designation, the federal government went into action acquiring the properties from the islands' owners. Island properties under public ownership were transferred to the federal government. Private property owners were given three options: outright purchase; continued usage under a 25-year lease arrangement; or usage of the property until the last living person on the deed died, at which time the land usage rights would expire. Some of the 25-year leases were not finalized until the early 1980s so these agreements have only recently expired. Today, only a few privately occupied parcels remain on Sand and Rocky Islands under the life-lease arrangements.

In 2004, a wilderness area was established in the park, encompassing about 80% of the land in the Apostle Islands National Lakeshore. This designation insures that the islands will not lose their wild and primitive character, but at the same time allows the public the access within the park they currently enjoy.

There are several important factors that have allowed the park to retain its wilderness appearance through the years. Most important is the intelligent administration of the National Park Service, supported by the community, which has followed wilderness principles, preventing any commercial exploitation of the islands. Another factor is the comparatively low number of visitors to the park, caused by the long winters. In addition, the lack of public transportation to the area and the absence of nearby interstate highways also result in fewer visitors. The park is simply not easy to get to. It's interesting to note that the projection of 920,000 seasonal visits set forth during the Congressional hearings on the park's establishment never materialized. The current level of annual visitation is approximately 200,000, and is not expected to rise significantly in future years. The reasons for this disparity in the numbers are several, including the fact that the planned scenic highway along the mainland shore portion of the park was never built. Critics of the park's establishment before the 1967 Senate Committee hearings pointed out that the type of fishing in the waters of the Apostle Islands (trolling) was not popular with sports fishermen; large boats were needed to boat safely among the islands; and the water was too cold for most recreational activities. These critics pointed out that more favorable areas for popular types of fishing, boating and other water-related activities existed on the mainland, south of the proposed park. These critics have been proven correct—to the benefit of today's current park visitors, since the waters, beaches and trails of the islands are uncrowded and provide the user with a wilderness experience.

In 2006, the Apostle Islands National Lakeshore was voted "the most pristine national park in the United States" by *National Geographic Traveler* magazine. The National Park Service, the citizens of the nearby communities and the returning visitors to the islands are united in their belief that future generations should continue to experience the "pristine" beauty of these islands.

APPENDIX III

THE KENNEDY CONNECTION

Senator John F. Kennedy made at least two trips to Ashland prior to his election as president. On one trip, in September 1959, Jacqueline Kennedy accompanied him. They both sat on a platform stand constructed in front of the Ashland County Courthouse on Main Street from which Kennedy spoke. Kennedy made another trip to the Ashland area on St. Patrick's Day, March 17, 1960, in his quest to win the Wisconsin Democratic primary for president. This trip is discussed in Theodore White's book *The Making of the President—1960*. At that time Wisconsin had one of the earliest primaries in the nation, making it an important election for anyone attempting to secure the Democratic nomination. His main opponent in the primaries was Senator Hubert Humphrey of Minnesota. Humphrey was favored to win Wisconsin, but Kennedy's efforts in the state paid off when he won.

Later, as president, he returned on September 24, 1963, one of the early stops he made during his last official trip as president, before he was assassinated. He flew into Duluth, Minnesota on the president's jetliner, *Air Force One*, and transferred to a helicopter. He flew over the Apostle Islands and was impressed with what he saw. He always had a love of water and sailed extensively. He followed up his flight over the islands with a speech extolling the area's natural resources to an estimated 10,000 cheering residents of the area at the Ashland airport. Wisconsin Senator Gaylord Nelson, a Kennedy supporter, and an important advocate of having the Apostle Islands declared a national park, accompanied him during this trip. The initial efforts designating the area as a national park were moving forward when the tragedy of Kennedy's assassination occurred less than two months later.

In recognition of Kennedy's visits to Ashland the airport was renamed the Kennedy Memorial Airport. The airport can be reached by going south off US 2 at Sanborn Avenue (the last stoplight), on the western edge of Ashland, approximately three miles. Today the airport is quiet and peaceful as only occasional private planes use its runways, a dramatic change from the day that President Kennedy spoke there.

In further recognition of the day that the president came to Ashland a 50th anniversary celebration was held at the airport on September 24, 2013. Although the crowd was significantly smaller than the one in 1963, numbering in the hundreds rather than the thousands, they heard stirring tributes to the president in addition to hearing his voice giving the speech he gave on that day fifty years earlier—much of it still relevant today.

An interesting footnote to the Kennedy connection to the area is that his son, John F. Kennedy, Jr., came to Bayfield with a group of friends in August 1995, staying at Gruenke's Inn, and did some kayaking among the islands.

On a more somber note, the black granite atop the grave of the president in Arlington National Cemetery came from a quarry near Mellen, about twenty-four miles south of Ashland. He had visited Mellen on the same day as his visit to Ashland in March 1960.

Senator Kennedy and his wife, Jacqueline, in Ashland
September 26, 1959

President Kennedy at the Ashland Airport
September 24, 1963

APPENDIX IV
HISTORIC MILESTONES
OF ASHLAND, WISCONSIN

Since Ashland was the center of activity for the northern area of Wisconsin for many years beginning in the mid-nineteenth century it is interesting to note the population trend and the major events that have occurred during that time.

Population trend:
    1860:   450 (Ashland County)
    1870:   211 (Ashland County)
    1880:   951 (Town of Ashland)
    1890: 9,956 (Town of Ashland)
    1900: 13,074 (City of Ashland)
    1905: 14,519 (City of Ashland)
    1910: 11,594 (City of Ashland)
    1920: 11,334 (City of Ashland)
    1930: 10,622 (City of Ashland)
    1940: 11,101 (City of Ashland)
    1950: 10,640 (City of Ashland)
    1960: 10,132 (City of Ashland)
    1970: 9,615 (City of Ashland)
    1980: 9,115 (City of Ashland)
    1990: 8,818 (City of Ashland)
    2000: 8,620 (City of Ashland)
    2010: 8,216 (City of Ashland)

Significant Events:
    1659 French explorers, Radisson and Groseilliers arrive in Chequamegon Bay and set up camp at the mouth of Fish Creek, west of Ashland.

    1854 Ojibwe (Chippewa) cede Wisconsin land to the United States.

    1887 Ashland formed.

83

1893 Electric street car begins operation, running down Main Street.

1896 Buffalo Bill Cody brings Chippewa and Sioux chiefs together to sign peace treaty, while touring with his Wild West show.

1903 First auto driven into town.

1903 Douglas MacArthur enters military service upon graduation from West Point giving Ashland as his official point of entrance. Apparently, his sponsor was a congressional representative from the area. There is no record of MacArthur ever being in Ashland.

1917 John Philip Sousa's band plays in Ashland.

1918 World War I ends. 31 Ashland men killed.

1922 Main Street paved with bricks.

1923 Fire department gives up horses for trucks.

1924 Tornado strikes west of city and kills six.

1928 President Calvin Coolidge visits city.

1929 Poet Carl Sandburg visits city.

1933 Highway US 2 becomes first concrete road in county.

1945 World War II ends. 64 Ashland men killed.

1948 Homecoming parade for Fleet Admiral William Leahy

1953 Korean War ends. 9 Ashland men killed.

1957 Northwestern ore docks close.

1959 Senator John F. Kennedy visits city
with his wife, Jacqueline.

1960 Senator Kennedy returns to Ashland prior to
Wisconsin primary election.

1963 John F. Kennedy returns to Ashland as
president and gives speech at airport.

1965 Soo Line ore dock closes after last shipment of
ore from Ashland.

1970 Last passenger train leaves Northwestern depot.

1975 Vietnam War ends. 4 Ashland men killed.

1987 Ashland celebrates 100th year anniversary.

2013 Last ore dock torn down.

SOURCES FOR ADDITIONAL INFORMATION

Apostle Islands

Holzhueter, John O., *Madeline Island and the Chequamegon Region,* Madison: The State Historical Society of Wisconsin, 1986. A historical review of Madeline Island and the surrounding region.

National Park Service, *A Guide to Apostle Islands National Lakeshore,* Washington: Department of Publications, U. S. Department of the Interior, 1988. Official National Park Handbook for the Apostle Islands National Lakeshore.

National Park Service, DVD/VHS, *On the Edge of Gichigami—Voices of the Apostle Islands,* Produced by Harper's Ferry Center (20 min).

Newman, Lawrence, *The Apostle Islands—America's Wilderness in the Water,* South Elgin: Silver Millennium Publications, Inc., 2012. A guide for boaters, kayakers, campers and beachcombers.

Newman, Lawrence, *Discovering the Apostle Islands,* South Elgin: Silver Millennium Publications, Inc., 2009, a tourist's guide to the Apostle Islands area, including recommended places to visit on the islands and the mainland.

Rennicke, Jeff, photographs by Layne Kennedy, *Jewels on the Water,* Friends of the Apostle Islands National Lakeshore, 2005. Photographic review of Apostle Islands history—both past and present.

Ross, Hamilton, *La Pointe: Village Outpost on Madeline Island*, Madison: State Historical Society, 2000. History of La Pointe and Madeline Island.

Strzok, Dave, *A Visitor's Guide to the Apostle Islands National Lakeshore,* Ashland: Superior Printing and Specialties, 1999. A comprehensive review of the islands and their history, including useful information for those boating, hiking and camping in the islands.

Official website for the Apostle Islands National Lakeshore: nps.gov/apis

Area Information
Ashland Area Chamber of Commerce
1716 Lake Shore Drive West
Ashland, WI 54806
715-682-2500/visitashland.com

Bayfield Chamber of Commerce and Visitor Bureau
42 S. Broad St.
Bayfield, WI 54814
715-779-3335 /bayfield.org

Madeline Island Chamber of Commerce
PO Box 274
La Pointe, WI 54850
715-747-2801/madelineisland.com

Washburn Area Chamber of Commerce
126 W. Bayfield St.
Washburn, WI 54891
715-373-5017

Big Top Chautauqua
3 miles south of Bayfield, west of Highway 13
715-373-5552/888-244-8368
www.bigtop.org

Camping—National Lakeshore
National Park Service
Apostle Islands National Lakeshore Headquarters
415 Washington Ave
Bayfield, WI 54814
715-779-3397/nps.gov/apis
Camping permits can be obtained in Bayfield or at the
National Park Service office in Little Sand Bay. Request
the brochure "Camping in the Apostle Islands".

Campgrounds
Apostle Islands Area Campground
½ mile south of Bayfield on Highway 13 & County J
715-779-5524

Big Bay State Park Madeline
Island
715-747-6425
Reservations must be made through Reserve America
    (reserveamerica.com) 888-947-2757

Big Bay Town Park
Madeline Island
1st come/1st served (Fee for use—
    payable at campground)

Buffalo Bay Campground and Marina
14669 Highway 13
Bayfield, WI 54814
715-779-3743

Dalrymple Campground
1 mile north of Bayfield on Highway 13
1st come/1st served (Fee for use—
    payable at campground)
Operated by City of Bayfield
www.cityofbayfield.com

Little Sand Bay Campground
715-779-5233
Operated by Town of Russell

MemorialPark
Washburn, WI
715-373-6174
Operated by Town of Washburn

Point Detour Campground
1st come/1st served (Fee for use—payable at
    campground). Operated by National Park Service.

West End Park
Washburn, WI
715-373-6174
Operated by Town of Washburn

Cruise Boats/Water Taxis/Ferry
Apostle Islands Cruise Service
City Dock, Bayfield, WI 54814
800-323-7619/715-779-3925
www.apostleisland.com

Apostle Trawlers
Island cruising
651-485-8989
apostletrawlers.com

Adventure Vacations
Water taxis and tours from Madeline Island
104 Middle Road
La Pointe, WI 5485
715-747-2100/866-910-0300

Ashland Boat Tours
Water taxis and island cruises
Ashland, WI 54806
715-292-5622

Nourse's Sport Fishing (Water taxi also)
100 Yacht Club Drive, end of 3rd St.
Bayfield, WI 54814
866-819-4330/715-779-3253
www.noursesfishing.com

Madeline Island Ferry Line
Summer hours: Every ½ hour during the day from
  both Bayfield and Madeline Island
715-747-2051
www.madferry.com

Fishing Charters
Angler's All (Captain Roger LaPenter)
2803 Lake Shore Drive East
Ashland,   WI   54806
715-682-5754
anglersallwisconsin.com

Black Hawk Fishing Charters (Captain Ken Nourse)
86800 Betzold Road
Bayfield, WI 54814
800-779-3261
blackhawkcharters.com

Dave's Fishing Charters (Captain Dave Sorenson)
PO Box 206
Ashland, WI 54806
715-682-3379
davesfishingcharters.com

Estain Sport Fishing (Captain Jody Estain)
715-292-5622

Nourse's Sport Fishing (Captain Laurie Nourse)
100 Yacht Club Drive, end of 3rd St.
Bayfield, WI 54814
866-819-4330/715-779-3253
www.noursefishing.com

River Rock Charters (Captain Scott Bretting)
1200 West Lake Shore Drive
Ashland, WI 54806
715-682-3232/715-292-1085
www.riverrockinn.net

Roberta's Sport Fishing Charters (Captain Tony Rippel)
PO Box 841
Bayfield, WI 54814
715-779-5744/888-806-0944
www.robertascharters.com

Hiking
National Park Service, *Hiker's Guide to Apostle Islands
National Lakeshore*, Edited by Neil Howk, Asst. Chief of
Resources Education, Apostle Islands National
Lakeshore, Fort Washington: Eastern National, 2001.

McKinney, John, *The Joy of Hiking: Hiking the Trailmaster Way*, Berkeley: Wilderness Press, 2005.

Website describing hiking trails in the islands: gorp.com/gorp/resource/us_ns/wi/hik_apo.html

<u>Kayaks/Canoes/Paddleboards</u>
Adventure Vacations-Madeline Island
104 Middle Road
La Pointe, WI 54850
715-747-2100/866-910-0300
www.Adv-Vac.com

Living Adventure Inc. (kayaks)
88260 State Highway 13
Bayfield WI 54814
715-779-9503/866-779-9503
www.livingadventure.com
Located 2 miles north of Bayfield in Red Cliff

Apostle Islands Kayaks-Madeline Island
715-747-3636
apostleislandskayaks.com

Wilderness Inquiry (kayaks)
33090 Little Sand Bay Rd.
Bayfield, WI 54814
800-728-0719/612-676-9400

Lost Creek Adventures and Outfitters
22475 Highway 13
Cornucopia, WI 54827
715-953-2223
lostcreekadventures.org

Trek & Trail (kayaks)
7 Washington Ave
Bayfield, WI 54814
800-354-8735/715-779-3595

Bog Lake Outfitters
Canoe and rowboat rentals
Big Bay Town Park, Madeline Island
715-747-2685

<u>Kennedy Connection</u>
White, Theodore H., *The Making of a President—1960*,
New York: Atheneum Publishers, 1961. (pp 83-86)

Film of President Kennedy's September 24-28, 1963 trip,
which included Ashland-last official trip of his presidency.
http://www.jfklibrary.org/AssetViewer/Archives/JFKWHF -
WHN07.aspx

<u>Lighthouses</u>
Strozk, Dave and Trapp, Nancy, *Lighthouses of the
Apostle Islands,* Bayfield: 2001.

Lighthouse Celebration Cruises (early September)
PO Box 990
Bayfield, WI 54814
800-779-4487
lighthousecelebration.com

Keeper of the Light
19 Front Street
Bayfield, WI 54814
800-779-4487
keeperofthelight.net
This store stocks a variety of nautical merchandise.

Museums

Ashland Historical Society Museum
509 W. Main Street
Ashland, WI 54806
715-682-4911
ashlandhistory.com

Bayfield Heritage Center
30 N. Broad Street
Bayfield, WI 54814
715-779-5958
bayfieldheritage.org

Bayfield Maritime Museum
131 S. 1st Street
Bayfield, WI 54814
715-779-9919

Cornucopia Historic Green Shed Museum Highway
13 at the Siskiwit Bay Harbor Cornucopia, WI 54827

Madeline Island Museum
226 Colonel Woods Ave.
La Pointe, WI 54850
715-747-2415/www.madelineislandmuseum.org

Washburn Cultural Center
1 E. Bayfield Street (State Highway 13) Washburn,
WI 54891
715-373-5591

National Park Service
Apostle Islands National Lakeshore Headquarters
415 Washington Ave
Bayfield, WI 54814 715-779-3397/nps.gov/apis

Native American History
Armstrong, Benjamin, *Early Life Among the Indians*, Press of A. W. Bowron, 1892. This out-of-print book can be downloaded from Google.

Northern Great Lakes Visitor Center
29270 County Road G
Ashland, WI 54806
715-685-9983
nglvc.org
Located on County Road G, ½ mile west of
  junction of US 2 and State Route 13, west of
  Ashland, WI

Restaurants
Delta Diner
14385 County Highway H
Delta, WI 54856
715-372-6666
www.deltadiner.com

Rittenhouse Inn
301 Rittenhouse Avenue
Bayfield, WI 54814
800-779-2129/715-779-5111
www.rittenhouseinn.com

The Platter Restaurant
315 Turner Road
Ashland, WI 54806
715-682-2626
www.thehistoricplatter.com

Portside Restaurant
34475 Port Superior Road
Bayfield, WI 54814
715-779-5360
www.BayfieldPortside.com

Greunke's First Street Inn
17 Rittenhouse Avenue
Bayfield, Wi 54814
715-779-5480
www.greunkesinn.com

El Dorado Restaurant
2320 Lake Shore Drive West
Ashland, WI 54806
715-682-9658
www.eldoradomexicancuisine.com

Rustic Roost
8355 U. S Highway 2
Iron River, WI 54857
715-372-4426

Sailboat Charters-Bareboat
Apostle Islands Yacht Charter Association
Madeline Island Yacht Club
715-747-2655

Superior Charters, Inc.
34475 Port Superior Road
Bayfield,WI 54814
715-779-5124
SuperiorCharters.com

Sailboat Charters-Captained
Animaashi Sailing Co.
888-272-4548/715-779-5468
animaashi.com

Madeline Island Yacht Club
633 Fort Road
La Pointe, WI 54850
715-747-2655

Dreamcatcher Sailing
100 Rittenhouse Avenue
Bayfield, Wi 54814
715-779-5561
www.howlinbayfield.com

Manitou Classic Sailing Charters
612-850-2981/612-750-5826
manitousailingcharters.com

Northern Breezes
763-542-9707
NorthernBreezesSchool.com

Superior Charters, Inc.
34475 Port Superior Rd Bayfield, WI 54814
715-779-5124
SuperiorCharters.com